WOW! It's always NOW!™

Written and Illustrated by Gil Toperoff

Acknowledgements

I want to thank neuroscientist and author Sam Harris
for his insightful speech entitled, Death and the Present Moment,
posted to YouTube. In his reference to time he states, "It is always now."
That phrase piqued my interest and helped inspire me
to write this children's book.

I'm also grateful to my granddaughter, Zoe Leah Toperoff
for suggesting key visuals such as a tape measure and a tutu
to convey how time measures our lives and how it moves
with such beauty and grace.

With love
for my grandchildren,
Zoe, Hannah, Wren and Watson

TICK TOCK! TICK TOCK! TICK TOCK! TICK TOCK

Tick tock! Tick tock!
Did you ever shake the hands of a clock?
Some hands are fast, others are slow
Measuring lives wherever they go.
But nothing can stop time's endless flow

TICK TOCK
OCK! TICK TOCK
TICK TOCK!
TICK TOCK!

ICK TOCK! TICK TOCK! TICK TOCK! TICK TOCK! TICK TOCK

16 15 14 13 12 11 10 9 8

TICK TOCK! TICK TOCK!

Wow! It's always now!

TICK TOCK! TICK TOCK! TICK TOCK! TICK TOCK

'Round in circles those clock hands race
While the past and the future keep running in place.
No matter how long it keeps up its pace
Time always moves with such beauty and grace.

CK TOCK

Wow! It's always now!

TICK **TOCK!** TICK **TOCK!** TICK **TOCK!** TICK **TOCK**

Yesterday's gone, tomorrow's not here
No matter how much they may try to appear.
Time does its magic year after year
Making our visible world disappear.

Wow! It's always now!

TICK **TOCK!** TICK **TOCK!** TICK **TOCK!** TICK **TOCK**

Open your eyes and what do you see?
Starlight streaming from in-fin-i-ty.
Each tiny glimmer of light from afar
Helps to reveal just who we are.

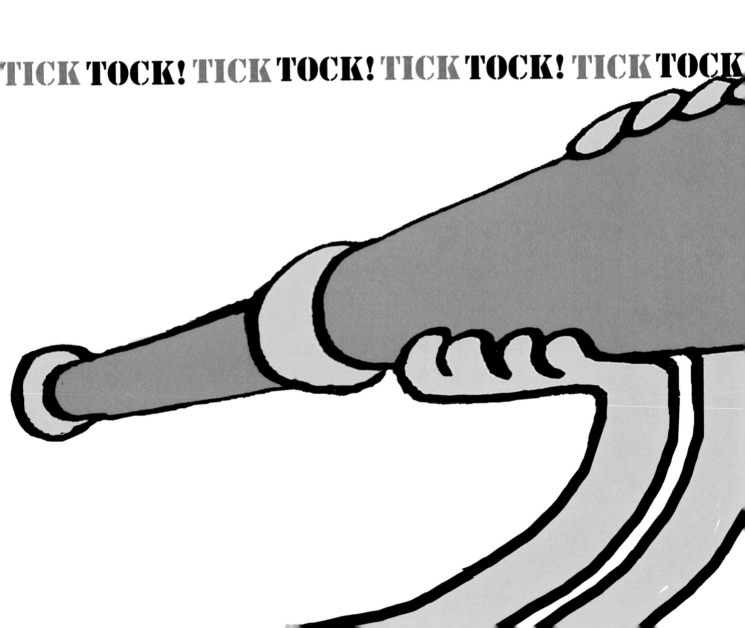

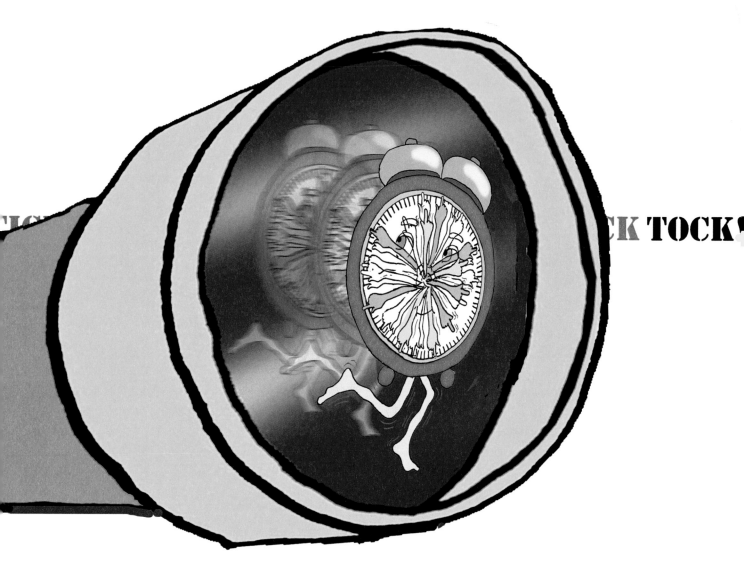

Wow! It's always now!

TICK TOCK! TICK TOCK! TICK TOCK! TICK TOCK

The past flies by in the wink of an eye
With memories stacked clear up to the sky
But all we can do is wave goodbye.

ICK TOCK! TICK TO... TOCK

Wow! It's always now!

TICK **TOCK!** TICK **TOCK!** TICK **TOCK!** TICK **TOCK**

The future stretches so far out in space
It's too hard to catch a glimpse of it's face.
Before you know it it's gone with no trace.

TICK TOCK! TICK TOCK! TICK TOCK! TICK TOCK!

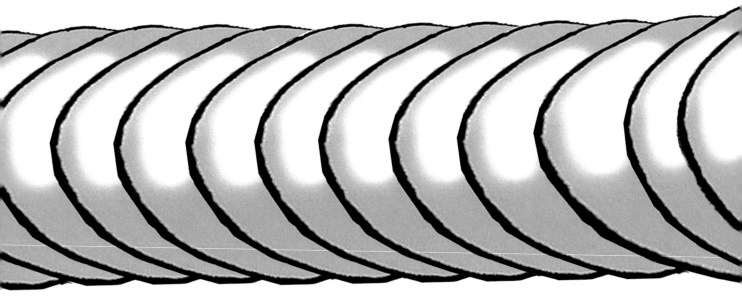

Wow! It's always now!

TICK TOCK! TICK TOCK! TICK TOCK! TICK TOCK

Eons come and eons go
Like waves washing up on the beach
Seeming to last forever,
Casting shadows so far out of reach.

TICK **TOCK!** TICK **TOCK!** TICK **TOCK!** TICK **TOCK!**

Don't put off all the things you might do
To some future day and place.
Time's always sneaking up on you
'Til it's staring you right in the face.

TICK **TOCK!** TICK **TOCK!** TICK **TOCK!** TICK **TOCK**

Treasure the time that you have on this earth
Savor each day you've had since your birth
Fill them with wisdom, and wonder and mirth
'Til each precious moment has infinite worth.

TICK TOCK! TICK TOCK! TICK TOCK! TICK TOCK!

Because .....
Wow! It's always now!

About the Author

Gil Toperoff was born in Philadelphia and first studied art in the studio of his uncle, Martin Jackson, a well known Philadelphia oil painter and print maker. After moving to Pittsburgh with his parents he continued his love of art by taking weekend classes at Carnegie Melon's Art School for Children.

Gil later majored in Fine Art at the University of Wisconsin in Madison and Advertising Design at the Art Center College of Design in Pasadena, California. Upon graduating he was hired as an art director by the Leo Burnett Advertising Agency in Chicago. Gil also worked at several other leading advertising and promotion agencies in the Chicago area. Eventually he became Creative Director on the McDonald's Family Marketing account at Frankel & Co., the top promotion agency in the country at that time. There, for over sixteen years he helped develop and promote a local unknown promotional concept called the Happy Meal into the most successful national promotion ever directed to kids and their families.

Soon after the birth of his first grandchild, Zoe, Gil wrote a short Valentine's Day poem for her and decided to illustrate it. *Follow Your Heart* became an expanded version of that poem and the title of his first children's book. He then wrote a second book entitled, *Wow! It's Always Now!* for Zoe and his three other grandchildren, Hannah, Wren and Watson.

Gil's surreal images are inspired and influenced by a variety of artists and illustrators including Peter Max, Alphonse Mucha, Maxfield Parrish, Keith Haring,, Salvadore Dali and M. C. Escher. Gil uses a fluid whimsical art style to create bold vibrant images that reinforce the universal themes in his poems. Anyone can benefit from many of his life experiences illustrated here. It's easy to see why his work has such strong appeal to both young and old alike.